# Motivation for Mompreneurs

### COMPILER~DR. M.E. PORTER

*Mompreneurs at Work*

She looks at land and buys it, and with money she has earned she plants a vineyard.
Proverbs 31:16

FOREWORD WRITTEN BY

DAWNIEL PATTERSON WINNINGHAM
AMERICA'S #1 "QUIT COACH"

Compiled by Dr. M.E. Porter

# *Motivation for Mompreneurs*
## *Mompreneurs at Work*

# Foreword By
# Dawniel Patterson Winningham

Soulidified Publishing LLC™, Atlanta, Georgia
*A Subsidiary of Pearly Gates Publishing LLC™*

## Motivation for Mompreneurs
## Mompreneurs at Work

Copyright © 2017
Dr. Marilyn E. Porter

All Rights Reserved.
No portion of this publication may be reproduced, stored in any electronic system, or transmitted in any form or by any means (electronic, mechanical, photocopy, recording, or otherwise) without written permission from the publisher. Brief quotations may be used in literary reviews.

Unless otherwise stated, all Scripture passages are taken from the King James Version (KJV) of the Holy Bible, Public Domain. Used by permission from Zondervan via Biblegateway.com.

ISBN 13: 978-1945117732
ISBN 10: 1945117737
Library of Congress Control Number: 2017941890

Published by:
*Soulidified Publishing LLC™*
A Christian Publisher located in Atlanta, Georgia (USA)

Compiled by Dr. M.E. Porter

## **DEDICATION**

This book is dedicated to

*EVERY*

Mompreneur around the globe!

## ACKNOWLEDGMENT

To my Trusty Sidekick:

Thank you for **ALWAYS** being there

to support your

*Scatter-Brained* friend.

Compiled by Dr. M.E. Porter

## FOREWORD

Moms can do **ANYTHING**. When they wrote the words to the 1970's jingle for Enjoli, "*I can bring home the bacon, fry it up in a pan - and NEVER let you forget you're a man...*", they ain't *NEVER* lied!

I think in some ways, being a mom makes you the ultimate juggler; and because you are the ultimate juggler, it makes you an **EXCELLENT** entrepreneur. You just have to translate those mothering skills to your role as an entrepreneur.

# Motivation for Mompreneurs

I know as well as anyone about the "juggle" of being a Mompreneur. Although I spent the majority of my "career" in corporate America, the juggle was still along the same lines. Having left corporate America two years ago and now managing a business that makes just over a half million dollars a year *(2017 will be our first million dollar+ year)* **AND** having to do it while being a single mother of three children, I *KNOW* that **YOU** have what it takes to do the same - or even better!

**Great moms are patient.** It takes *patience* to be an amazing entrepreneur. None of this happens overnight. Everything is a process; just like your children growing up and learning, you have to do the same as an entrepreneur. Your business **MUST** experience growing pains. There is no way around it. Be patient.

Compiled by Dr. M.E. Porter

**Great moms remain positive.** Every day of raising your children wasn't always the best day. Trust me: You will have down days in your business as well. The secret is to *STAY POSITIVE*, even when things don't look so good. You **KNOW** that this, *TOO*, shall pass. It did with the children, and it will with your business.

**Moms understand the importance of discipline.** Lack of discipline is what derails most entrepreneurs. Never forget the structure and order it took for you to raise your family. It takes that much and **MORE** to keep your business on track.

**Have a sense of humor.** I recall a time I had my twins fully-dressed, and Hope grabbed a bowl of oatmeal from the counter and turned it over on Faith's head…*JUST* as we were heading out the door for daycare and work. I had the choice: laugh or cry. I laughed. We **STILL** laugh about it to this day. There will be days in your business when you have to choose to laugh or cry. How about another quick tryst down Memory Lane? One day, I took off my wig (on accident) in front of **hundreds** of people online. I laughed! Not only did I laugh, I left the video up as **PROOF** that sometimes, you just can't take yourself too seriously.

Compiled by Dr. M.E. Porter

**Do the BEST you can and learn as you go.** I remember bringing home Tyler from the hospital…knowing *NOTHING*…but I learned. So, when I got pregnant again, I thought I had that one in the bag. Well, I was pregnant with **TWINS**! So, *BACK* to the drawing board I went to learn even more! I made it, though. Don't close yourself off from the **EXPERT** advice that is available in the world. The **MORE** you are willing to learn, the *more* your business grows! My current earnings are directly on pace with the investments I've made to learn and grow my business.

# Motivation for Mompreneurs

**Set boundaries.** When the children were growing up, they had areas that were off limits to their toys, shoes, and clothes. Venturing outside of those boundaries got their stuff thrown in the trash. As women, while we may *WANT* to help everyone on this journey, if we don't set boundaries, **WE** will end up failing ourselves. When people are *OUT* of bounds, throw their stuff in the trash; meaning don't respond to it or go out of your way to take care of it.

**Know your worth.** I *KNOW* I did a great job raising my children. It wasn't always my 100%, but I did what I could. There is **NO** Mother's Day card or box of chocolates that can pay me back for the energy and effort I expended while raising my children. It's the same with my business. I know my worth - and I don't hesitate to charge for it. Please **KNOW** that your gift to the world in the form of your business is worth *WHATEVER* you decide to charge. Stand by your prices. Forget the naysayers who would never buy your stuff anyway!

Compiled by Dr. M.E. Porter

Run your business like you run motherhood, and you will be okay. You have already accomplished one of the hardest jobs known to man.

You brought **LIFE** onto this planet. After that, birthing a business is *EASY* in comparison.

*~ Dawniel Patterson Winningham ~*
America's #1 Quit Coach
Helping women generate the *MONEY* they need to
**QUIT** their jobs.
Follow Dawniel on Twitter & Periscope
@wealthspeaker
Learn *MORE* about Quitting **YOUR** job at:
www.iamdawnielwinningham.com
Join me *LIVE* on Facebook **DAILY** for
tips and tricks to get you **FURTHER** towards
building your business:
www.facebook.com/dawnielwinningham

# It Takes a Strong Woman to Understand
*Tribute to My Mompreneur*

To understand that even though he's not right for her, her daughter needs a man in her life - a father figure.

To understand that you have to let your child overcome some things, even when you - as a mom - already have the answers.

It takes a strong woman to understand that she has to find her own path - even though she already knows it.

It takes a strong woman to allow her child's gifts to develop - even if she knows that sometimes, your relationship will suffer.

Sometimes, when I write about you, my words get stuck because I feel like writing words for you just isn't enough. Even though you're not at your final destination, living up to you is tough; but what better way to honor your mother than with the gifts that God gave you to serve?

Although it'll never be enough;
Even though I could never pay you back,
Sometimes the words don't come.
Sometimes they come out wrong.

## Compiled by Dr. M.E. Porter

Since I was young, the words are always different,
But the message the same:
Even on your "off" days,
You never get an off day.

So, although this isn't it
And I'll always strive to make you prouder,
I just wanted to make a public declaration
That I love you.

A mother like mine is very rare.
A woman who will run to your rescue, no matter how old you get - whether you deserve it or not.
I know this isn't long or elaborate, but it doesn't take many words to describe an indescribable woman.

She always made sure we had what we needed - and even **WANTED**. She sacrificed her life so many times to make sure we had a good one - and she's still doing it, even though all of her children are old enough to make their own sensible decisions. For that, she will always be an amazing woman.

Marilyn Elizabeth is a gift, a gem, and a woman of God who is beyond words.

I love you, Mom.

The 2nd Child (the one in the middle)
*~ Christina ~*

*"Her children rise up and call her blessed..."*

Proverbs 31:28

Compiled by Dr. M.E. Porter

## TABLE OF CONTENTS

| | |
|---|---|
| DEDICATION | VI |
| ACKNOWLEDGMENT | VII |
| FOREWORD | VIII |
| IT TAKES A STRONG WOMAN TO UNDERSTAND | XV |
| M.E.'S STRUGGLE | 1 |
| SPLIT IN TWO | 12 |
| SHARLRITA'S STRUGGLE | 23 |
| MS. JENNIFER PINK'S STRUGGLE | 30 |
| MY WAKE-UP CALL TO MOMPRENEURSHIP | 40 |
| MY STRUGGLE AS A MOMPRENEUR | 54 |
| JUGGLING FITNESS AND BEING A SINGLE MOM | 65 |
| THE CORNS SPEAK | 72 |
| CONTACT DR. MARILYN E. PORTER | 85 |
| OTHER M.E. PORTER TITLES | 86 |

Motivation for Mompreneurs

## **M. E.'s Struggle**
By Dr. M.E. Porter

My entrepreneurial journey developed very naturally. I was running a business before I began to *CALL* it a business. It was something I did very well, and people paid me for it. So, there shouldn't have been any struggle involved, right? **WRONG!**

There were days when I would realize I had been glued to the computer and telephone from sun up to sun down, and my own needs had not been met. I would forget to eat at times, and I do believe I missed a few showers here and there *(that's the truth)*. Even moreso, I would realize that my children had gone to school, come home, and would be back in the bed - and I had not so much as asked them how their day was.

**NO BUENO, MOM!**

## Compiled by Dr. M.E. Porter

Putting self and family first (after God, of course) was the struggle of my beginning…and sometimes my now.

I suppose one could say I was always a Mompreneur of sorts. I rarely worked outside of the home after my first daughter was born in 1992, yet I always had a "hustle". I knew how to generate income outside of the standard "9 to 5". The entrepreneurial spirit was in me. If I am honest, I do believe it developed in me as a child.

I used to see the drug dealers in my neighborhood (who were using the skills of an entrepreneur outside of the law) run **very** successful, self-motivated organizations that met the needs of their ideal customers.

# Motivation for Mompreneurs

I have always had the ability to take the lesson from **any** situation I am exposed to, and seeing those unlawful businessmen create *AND* sustain their profitable lifestyles sent the message to me that one can get up every day, **NOT** put on a suit, **NOT** leave the home, **NOR** be confined to the rules and regulations of someone else's workplace and make it. *However,* I knew that I was not divinely-designed for prison; so, although I paid close attention to their ability to build and rebuild, I would have to figure out how to translate that into a means of translating those skills into law-abiding businesses. I knew for certain one could live well outside of corporate America.

Being an entrepreneur is as natural to me as being a mom - which is why I must be aware of how much time I spend building my business and **always** remember I must build up my family as well.

Compiled by Dr. M.E. Porter

**M.E.'s Motivation**

"*Good morning, Lord. Thank you for this new day filled with new mercies, new ideas, and a dose of wisdom!*"

My days begin with giving love and gratitude to The Creator of ME, my family, and my business.

> "*O God, You are my God;*
> ***Early will I seek You;***
> *My soul thirsts for You;*
> *My flesh longs for You*
> *In a dry and thirsty land*
> *Where there is no water.*"
> *Psalm 63:1*

# Motivation for Mompreneurs

Notice the Scripture says "...*early will I seek you*..." I rise with the knowledge that if I do not seek the hand and support of the Holy Spirit the **moment** I become conscious in the morning, my day will begin with me effortlessly doing what comes natural to me - *BUT* I will have no intentional breaks in my day.

Seeking God first - "*Seek ye first the Kingdom of God...*" (Matthew 6:33) - helps me move in wisdom throughout the day. I can wake up and go **HARD!** My mind functions at warp speed. I wake up with new ideas *as well as* the answers from the day before that I may have missed, so I *MUST* seek the face of a loving God before I unleash myself on my family or business.

I encourage you to do the same.

*****

Compiled by Dr. M.E. Porter

*Dear Mompreneur,*

*Your children are blessed and blessed to call you 'Mom'. If you are a wife to a husband, you are indeed his good thing. Your clients are blessed to have your skills, talents, and abilities working in their lives.*

*My Beloved Sister, I am writing that I might remind you of this one thing:* **YOU** *need* **YOU**, *too. Start your day off with surrender to The One who created you to be your fabulous self. That is how you ensure God is glorified.* **YOU** *are grounded, and everyone else you are to serve in your day will be blessed by your hands.*

*Sincerely,*
*Marilyn*

*"She makes tapestry for herself; her clothing is fine linen and purple."*
Proverbs 31:22

Motivation for Mompreneurs

## This is Dedicated to the Ones I Love

**YOU** changed my life. Yes, **YOU** - First child. My point of view about life in general changed the moment my body assured me you would be the one to exit my womb first. There were others who occupied my womb before you, but their stories ended before they had the opportunity to enter the earthspace as living, breathing beings. But **YOU**? **YOU** were a fighter from conception. Thank you for allowing me to mother you into your greatness. Thank you for being my *first* reason to tap into my own greatness.

**"MJD"**

**YOU** filled my life. Yes, **YOU** - Second child. You renewed the fire inside of me that began to burn with a low flame. From the womb, you caused me to hunger for me (*sometimes literally...I am sure you have heard the story of the Big Mac **and** Double Cheeseburger*). You made me remember that I was created to be big, bold, and rebellious - when necessary. Teaching you how to be confidently **YOU** taught me how to operate securely in my calling as a mother.

**"CDW (1)"**

**YOU** renewed my faith and ability to love. Yes, **YOU** - Third child. My life felt a little stale the months (perhaps *YEARS*) before I received word that you would be arriving. I didn't expect you, but I needed you to remind me that God is faithful. Even now, I remember the doctor telling me that you may have some respiratory issues due to a medication I had to have while pregnant with you. Then, I quickly recall hearing the voice of God speak to my heart: *"Name her 'Charity' because she will be a reminder to you that I love you and you need to love yourself."* Every day since I met **YOU** on January 18, 2002, you have been a reminder of God's faith and love towards me. Thank you for representing God's love for me.
**"CDW (2)"**

*To My Babies in Heaven:* You all have my DNA, so I know you are **all** having a Praise Party! Kiss Jesus for me!

Compiled by Dr. M.E. Porter

M.E. Porter is the CEO of the Soul INpowerment Group - which houses Soulidified Publishing (her publishing house), The Soul Restoration Center (where she is the Pastor), and The Pink Pulpit Crusade International.

M.E. is the biological mother of three beautiful daughters and the Spiritual Mother to many others. Learn more by visiting:
www.marilyneporter.com.

## MOMPRENEUR MOTIVATOR

"Accept responsibility for your life. Know that it is you who will get you where you want to go; no one else."

~ Les Brown ~

Compiled by Dr. M.E. Porter

## Split in Two
By Kristen Rogers

**Struggle:** *To make forceful or violent efforts* **TO GET FREE** *of restraint or constriction.*

I was born into the struggle of the best of both worlds. My mother and father lived two separate lives, but both offered me valuable life skills from two different playing fields. My mother gave her life to Christ by the time I was born. My father? He decided against doing so.

So, there I was: born naturally into one world, but subconsciously being divided into two.

## Motivation for Mompreneurs

I had a mother who taught me that miracles happen and checks pop up in the mail - when you have *faith*. I had a father who said, "If you don't do it, nobody else will." Although they raised me separately, they both played by the rules that were one in the same: "*Faith without works is dead*" (James 2:17). I witnessed my mother fight with poverty. Money in our household was not an option because money was not easily-accessible. When we did have it, it was hard to keep. I heard her pray and cry, pleading with God to provide a way of escape from a "broken spirit". I then saw the blessings come. Just as quickly, I watched the blessings go. As a child, I questioned it and quickly learned it was not a matter of blessings coming and going; it had everything to do with the *mentality* of the person who obtained the blessing.

Compiled by Dr. M.E. Porter

When I spent time with my father, he taught me (by example) how to be a **boss**. He was a businessman who provided for me *everything* I wanted and needed. Unfortunately, it was while *only* in his home. I watched my father work hard - late nights and early mornings, both legally…and illegally. I listened to him negotiate over the phone with his clients. He would ask me for advice on how to deal with them. "If you were me, what would you say?" This taught me how to think quickly. He would say, "Come on now! Think fast! Money don't wait for nobody!"

On Saturday mornings, my dad would give me a chore before I could play outside. It wasn't your average chore (like washing dishes). *MY* chore was counting his money. He would then have his best friend (who was a mathematician) come over and train me in numbers.

At the end of my math lesson every Saturday, he would give me $100.00 for my work and say, "Don't spend it all in one place!" or "Don't let this money burn a hole in your pocket!" He had **NO** idea I would go home to my mom on Sunday evenings and give her the money I had left over from the weekend. My dad was right: That money would burn holes in our pockets!

Unfortunately, as I grew older, I kept the same hole in my pocket. I was addicted to the culture of spending which says, "Spend to show that you have it, but when you need it, beg and plead with God and man for it."

That was my struggle; being addicted to the culture of spending. It played a **major** part in my upbringing. Ultimately, I spent more time with my mother than I did with my father, so I adapted to her way of living.

Daily, I would wake up and go to a job that paid me millions of dollars **LESS** than what I needed to start my own business - or so I thought. I began looking for other jobs and taking the ones that offered me more money. Still, I would continue finding myself in the same situation: not having enough money to start my own business. One day, I decided to create a monthly budget. In the budget, I wrote out **$800.00** worth of unnecessary "necessities". Something then happened. The entrepreneurial switch in my brain turned on! It was then I realized it wasn't my place of employment that needed to change. It wasn't more money that I needed.

My *mentality* needed an upgrade!

I then challenged myself to change the way I thought in order to change the way I live. I soon began to ditch the culture of spending and began to tell myself, "Sacrifice like others **won't** so that you can spend the rest of your life like others **can't**. Temporary satisfaction versus generational success." My life changed! The two worlds in which I had once lived separately had finally collided. It all made sense! My faith in my ability to become a great entrepreneur was determined by my works and the sacrifices I was willing to make in order to bring my dream to reality.

## Compiled by Dr. M.E. Porter

I encourage you to take a step outside of yourself. Have a heart-to-heart talk with the entrepreneur within you, **BUT** let the entrepreneur speak *FIRST*. I think the first thing it will tell you is to change the things that you can change. It starts with you. Be realistic about your current lifestyle and be truthful to your own self about your money. Live within the means for where you currently are. Saying "no" is vital on your journey to entrepreneurship, as it will help you focus on the bigger picture: **GENERATIONAL SUCCESS!**

I define generational success as this: Work hard and sacrifice today so that your children and those who come after can benefit from the hard work you've put in - while *THEY* continue to carry on the legacy by adding levels to the empire. **You have to struggle with it!** Be violent about what's yours! It's *YOUR* dream and *YOUR* future. Set your mind free from being restrained by a mentality that tells you to spend now, beg later. Being broke is not a spirit, but it can become a generational habit if **YOU** don't change.

> *"She considers a field and buys it;*
> *from her profits, she plants a vineyard"*
> Proverbs 31:16

Compiled by Dr. M.E. Porter

## Dedication to Lil D

Never would I have imagined that birthing you in such an unorthodox way would bring me to conceive and birth my own gifts. God sent you to me at the most opportune time. You've been my Moses, my way of escape, and my bold, little leader.

This is for you, Lil D.

Kristen Rogers is 29 years old and resides in Oakland, California. She is a mother and a writer. Learn more by visiting:
www.hergoldensole.com

Compiled by Dr. M.E. Porter

*"For I know the plans I have for you, declares the LORD, plans for welfare and not for evil, to give you a future and a hope"*
Jeremiah 29:11

Relax...with a warm bubble bath.

## Sharlrita's Struggle
By Sharlrita Deloatch

I didn't just jump into entrepreneurship; I was kind of **PUSHED** into it. About 12 years ago, I found myself in the back of a police car. The officer drove me to the police station where I was fingerprinted, booked, and labeled a convicted felon. At the time, I had no children; hence, my only accountability was to myself. At that time in my life, I didn't think much of me. That all changed in 2005 when I birthed my first child, Zaniyah.

Fast forward to 2014. I was feeling the residue from the felony being on my record. In 2012, I lost the job I had for over six years. I truly felt I had no purpose and really didn't know who I was in Christ. You can likely imagine the life I was living from 2012 to 2014…two years of being lost, confused, and lifeless.

After overcoming depression and my family and me coming out of homelessness, I guess you can say I had a "coming to Jesus moment" when He let me know in His loving way how important it is for me to walk in purpose. There were so many women waiting on my story, business, and all that I had to offer. He told me, "*Open your mouth*"; so, I decided to do just that.

I began working with a coach and decided to start my speaking career. It wasn't easy at all. I had to find my voice and be okay with sharing my story about being a convicted felon. In the beginning, I had no direction nor clarity about who I wanted to speak with. I allowed procrastination and fear to keep my career in speaking to get stale in 2015. All of a sudden, I stopped doing **anything** related to my business. I struggled with if I was good enough, if my voice mattered, and questioned, "*Would anyone really want to listen to me?*"

Then, I had to consider the well-being of my four children God gave me and the opportunity to be their mother.

*I had to rethink this entrepreneurship thing...*

I know I had to do it. I had to be fully-committed to my purpose on this earth. My children's lives and legacies depended on it. I became determined to leave my name and voice on this earth. When my name is mentioned, doors will open for them because they're **MY** seeds. I allow them to watch me go through my process. I allow them to see me truly live my life the way God wants me to. I allow them to see me walk with purpose - and do it passionately and unapologetically. When they have their children, they will be able to say, "That's my mommy - the woman who never gave up on her dreams!"

Compiled by Dr. M.E. Porter

**Sharlrita's Motivation**

I want to encourage you: No matter what, you can live the life of your dreams. It will take work and **so much** dedication from you to get it done. Use your story to help others overcome. Use your past to make you money…not stressed. I don't care *WHAT* you have been through; you **can** overcome and boldly tell your story to others. You're robbing not only yourself of greatness, but also those who are waiting on you to show up. I need you to show up proudly and boldly. That is your obligation. Look at your children. You owe them that much! Your legacy awaits!

> *"She girds herself with strength,*
> *and strengthens her arms."*
> Proverbs 31:17

## Dedication

I was always the one in my group of friends, at home, or even at church saying, "I will **NEVER** have any children!" Well, look at what God did! He gave me *four* beautiful souls. He gave me *four* blessings. I love you all so much and want you to know that you're my reason why I do what I do. You're why I keep pushing. You complete me, and I love you soooo much!

My four heartbeats: Zaniyah Russell, Antasia Deloatch, Caleb Deloatch, and Anthony 'AJ' Deloatch, Jr.

Love,
Mommy

Compiled by Dr. M.E. Porter

Servant. Wife. Mother. Speaker. Author. Coach. Mentor.
Learn more by visiting:
www.sharlritaspeaks.com.

## MOMPRENEUR MOTIVATOR

"Challenges are what make life interesting, and overcoming them is what makes life meaningful."

~ Joshua J. Marine ~

Compiled by Dr. M.E. Porter

## Ms. Jennifer Pink's Struggle
By Ms. Jennifer Pink

When you're a mother, you are supposed to focus on your children. You are supposed to do whatever it takes to make their lives better. For the majority of society, that means going to work, providing food and shelter, and (most importantly) putting yourself, your dreams, your desires, and your goals last.

Well, when you are a **single** mom, society believes you have to do all of those things…*times TWO*.

# Motivation for Mompreneurs

As a single mom of three, it seems like the whole world was finally at peace when I started my career with Los Angeles County. The more I climbed the ladder, the happier "they" became. What was most important: Making *them* happy or doing something that would make **ME** happy? I, of course, am a mother first and foremost, so taking care of my children, making sure they eat, have a place to live, and are always happy is **always** the priority.

What about going after *MY* dreams? What about living out *MY* purpose in life? Do I let all of that go if climbing the corporate ladder isn't in alignment with following *MY* purpose?

I tried to do what most of us do. I tried do both: climb the ladder for security and to appease "them" while going after my dreams. It sorta-kinda worked…for a little while. I was progressing in my career and going after my purpose on the side. Most of "them" thought I should be saving my money - not investing in a business. Most of "them" thought I should be spending more time with my children.

**I'm a single mother of three! All I do is spend time with my children!**

Instead of spending money on the latest Jordans and frivolous things, I invested into my children's future - into building a legacy for them. No matter how I tried to show "them" what I was doing or explain the importance of fulfilling my purpose, the more "they" refused to understand. The business was fulfilling my purpose. It was making me a better woman and mother. It was the best way I could provide for my children because they needed more than the basics of life; they, too, needed to learn how to **THRIVE**!

When this single mom of three decided to leave her career that seemed to be going nowhere but up, move across the country from California to Georgia with nothing but her, two of the children, and what could be packed in her car, "they" **KNEW** I had surely lost my mind. I tried to explain I was doing what I was called to do: I was going to live my life for God and make the impact on this world that He created me for. There was literally only **FIVE PEOPLE** in support of my decision.

## Compiled by Dr. M.E. Porter

For me, the hardest part about being a Mompreneur is going against what "they" said and thought. Even after I made the move, I still had to constantly deal with "them" telling me I made the wrong move, wasn't doing right by my children, and consistently being asked when I was going to give up on my passion and get a *job*. I have struggled in my life - more than once or twice - but the hardest struggle is having the faith to keep going on my journey to build the business/platform that I've been called to, even when I have no support, when "they" are all against me, and while I struggled financially as I started over.

To be honest, there are days I question whether or not I made the right choice.

*Am I being selfish? Am I sacrificing my children for my happiness?*

## Motivation for Mompreneurs

At the end of the day, I have to stay true to myself. I have to do what makes me whole because I can't serve my children, clients, nor anyone else unless I am whole. I get through the hard days. I get past what "they" say and think - by being **honest**. First and foremost, I admit and own up to my frustration, pain, hurt, and anger. After I admit those things, I make them my *fuel*. I allow it to force me to do what I've set out to accomplish. When the tide turns and things are working out and in my favor, I don't let go of those feelings or fuel because as long as I'm living, I have more purpose to fulfill.

*"She stretches out her hands to the distaff, and her hand holds the spindle."*
Proverbs 31:19

Compiled by Dr. M.E. Porter

## Dedication to The J Crew

I know we've gone through so many ups and downs along our journey to greatness. I know you've seen me fall, at my worst, and almost destroyed. I know the sacrifices you've made on behalf of me. I promise you that I love you with all my heart and would give everything and anything to and for each and every one of you. You each have blessed my life in a way like no other, and I wouldn't change any of you.

**Jocie,**
You are your grandmother's child. My biggest dream for you is for you to live out your dream and supersede my wildest expectations. Don't make the mistakes of those who have come before you. Be wise enough to learn from them. Stay true to you, but become a better you!

**Justin,**
You are my son. I love you - and don't let anyone tell you anything different. I want the best for you. I want you to become an amazing man. I will always fight for you, but won't hesitate to teach and correct you. No matter where I am in this world, you can always call it 'home'.

**Josiah,**
My catalyst for change! The baby who saved me from myself and also brought me to Jesus so I could truly be healed. I pray that you live up to the name God gave you - for more people than just me. You will be exactly who He has purposed you to be, as long as you keep after Him with everything.

**J'adore,**
You are my "love child". You were created by parents who truly love one another. For the first time in my life, I love myself and have experienced genuine love - thanks to your father. You are a product of our passion, molded perfectly by God's hands to BE love. Welcome to the world! All four corners of the earth need the love that radiates from your very being.

Blessings and Love to **all** of the JCrew!

Compiled by Dr. M.E. Porter

Servant Leader. Wife. Mother. Single Mom Coach. CEO.

Learn more by visiting:
www.thepinkfoundation.org

*"The **LORD** your God is in your midst, a mighty one who will save; He will rejoice over you with gladness; He will quiet you by His love; He will exult over you with loud singing."*
Zephaniah 3:17

Relax...by enjoying your favorite meal and a glass of wine.

Compiled by Dr. M.E. Porter

## My Wake-Up Call to Mompreneurship
By Pastor Maggy Reed

At a very young age, I knew I was a humanitarian. Helping people was just normal for me to step into. It was my passion. I had no problem serving. That's why I founded KaribAmerica's Well-Being Foundation, Inc. - a not-for-profit promoting health and wellness through nutrition. However, the core reason why I created it was to provide support to women with minor children - women who are affected by terminal diseases, such as cancer and HIV/AIDS.

I wanted to help provide support to mothers affected by cancer after I met a woman at work in 2008. She was married for 18 years and had three children, the oldest being 16 years old at the time. Her mammogram was due, and the results were heartbreaking: She had to have a double mastectomy immediately. She came to have her PET/CT done. As they were applying her IV, she confided in me that her husband had left her right when she needed him the most.

***I thought that was horrible!***

## Compiled by Dr. M.E. Porter

I **had** to create an organization in my community to help others like her to face that challenge in their lives. She told me she had no one to talk to, especially in her native language. I founded KaribAmerica for Caribbean American on May 13, 2009. I was pleased to meet medical professionals in the community, but one day, my supervisor called me into the office. I was laid off the **same** day without warning. I was heartbroken. I had children to care for without any other financial help at that time.

I **had** to find a way to provide for my family.

At the time, I already registered two patents for breast imaging patients and had the not-for-profit. Something told me there was more to that because I was asked earlier to give them my prototype so they can make more to use on their table. They didn't like my response. I told them the prototype was at the lawyer's office. Well, that was enough to get me out of there! Not too bright... Finances are needed to manufacture products, so if I'm struggling financially, I may not reach the success I was so happy about at the time. That's why they let me go, but **GOD** had other plans. I'm still an inventor and it is safe at the United States Patent and Trademark Office!

To become the entrepreneur I desired to be, I had to return to school because I needed a new mindset. I went and obtained a degree in Business Management, focused on marketing, public relations, and events.

It was a struggle to balance things in my life because I had no one to coach me at that time on how to make money. I only knew how to be excellent making somebody **else** rich and growing somebody **else's** dream. I do, however, thank *GOD* for the lessons learned.

I had to create a for-profit company - and I did! My mindset was slowly changing, and my children learned how to do simple things during Summer months like printing with us; however, I was not making enough to survive with all of the expenses I had.

*Here is what I did to keep myself motivated as a Mompreneur:* I had no time to become depressed. I had two young men to care for and ensure they had a secure future. One thing's for sure: I wanted to be there for them in their teenage years when they needed their parents the most.

So, I needed peace in the house to welcome the presence of God in order to understand what my next steps would be.

I talked to my children so that they understood the struggle I was dealing with and the sacrifices mom was about to make. I explained that I needed their cooperation. They literally followed my orders and kept the house in peace and in order.

*Here is what I did to encourage peace in my household:* I know that boys **love** to fight, so I eliminated anything that could cause them to fight and argue. I assigned them their own colors, too. Ben has his color. Toothbrush, sheets, plates, towels, deodorants, cups, water bottles, book bags, undershirts, toys…**all** were the same color. I did the same for Bryan. To this day, there is never a fight at home because it's color-coded. The only thing that was one color was their socks, and there is no fight about black socks.

I learned what to do to keep a child calm. It prevented me from having to go to school because of fights, which were nonexistent. I used lotions and soaps to relax and calm my children. I eliminated soda and junk food from their diet and replaced them with healthier foods to prevent chemical imbalance. I did what I had to do to keep the peace going in the household. I thank God for wisdom. God knows I couldn't handle anymore chaos in my life!

Throughout the years, I taught my sons to help with chores, such as prep a screen, clean it, set the garment on the printing table, print on it, and packaging - which made me proud of them.

Today, my sons are young adults. The chaotic years are over.

They really love to see my evolution over the years and how resilient I am when it comes to business. They have seen me fail many times. I'm glad about that - in a way. They learned that success takes work, and sometimes, failing is another way to discover other means to achieve success: perseverance, endurance, determination, and faith in God are needed to make it in this life.

I teach my sons that **every** move needs to be a giant, killer move. It needs to be a spiritual move, bold move, and courageous move. God loves a courageous person, and He *will* strengthen you if you faint not; He will renew you like an eagle.

I teach my sons the power of prayer and how to rely on God for success because He is *The One* to promote us in due time.

*"God is a sun and shield; the LORD gives grace and glory; no good thing does He withhold from those who walk uprightly."*

Psalm 84:11

Financially, it was a struggle. I never stopped praying for my children and our well-being. I asked God to protect them from people who can deter them from where God wants them to be. I prayed for their friends and other teenagers with influence on their lives. I know if anything happens to them while I'm figuring out how to serve in my business, I will not be focused…then it may cost me many delays.

Being an entrepreneur is not easy, but the earlier one is coached about their strengths and weaknesses, identify who they are here to serve, and being intentional in all areas of life, they **CAN** make it.

## Motivation for Mompreneurs

I encourage every woman reading this to create a blueprint - a pattern - for your children to follow, and keep the peace flowing in the family. It's needed if you want to be focused on building your business.

Have faith in God and pray constantly with your family so God can enlarge your territory to prosper you and the fruits of your hands.

Time management is very important as well. Prioritize the most important to the least important. Use your time wisely, and stay away from procrastination.

Be committed to reach your goal in spite of everything that may come your way - and stay away from other people's issues.

Learn the skills you need to take you to the next level. Hire a coach, and make wiser decisions in your financial life.

Cultivate patience during your learning process. Nurture the gifts God implanted within you. Appreciate small beginnings. Trust in God every step to reach the success promised unto you in Jeremiah 29:11.

You are already a victorious woman! God knitted you together in your mother's womb for a time like this.

Now, go, Woman of God. Be prosperous in this land, in Jesus' name!

> *"She perceives that her merchandise is good,
> and her lamp does not go out by night."*
> Proverbs 31:18

## Dedication

Mother to Ben and Bryan.

Motherhood is a gift that was given unto me when I least expected it. I thank God for Ben and Bryan. They taught me how to never give up in life in very difficult times. They cultivate my patience on a daily basis, but they never complained about anything.

**Ben**, my oldest, is a determined young man and a Wellness Coach, following my steps helping people live a healthier lifestyle.

**Bryan**, my youngest, is a happy, young man, very laid back, calm, and serene. I can see a Psychologist in him.

Compiled by Dr. M.E. Porter

Maggy Reed is a lover of life and arts.

Mother. Pastor. Author. Publisher. Medical Inventor/Innovator. Multilingual Speaker. Clergy. Life Coach. Social Entrepreneur. Humanitarian. Learn more by visiting:
http://bit.ly/inscribeitpublishing

# MOMPRENEUR MOTIVATOR

"The best revenge is massive success."

~ Frank Sinatra ~

Compiled by Dr. M.E. Porter

## My Struggle as a Mompreneur
By Sharon Covington Shamburger

When asked what my biggest struggle as a Mompreneur is, I immediately thought of *BALANCE*. Not only am I a mother who is building my own business; I work a full-time job as well. Balance can be difficult, but it is obtainable. Allow me to give you some insight into a typical day of mine - at least before I realized I had to work on my balance.

Mornings would begin at 5:00 a.m. in my home. That was time to prepare my children for school and myself for work. My daughter and son both had to be dropped off my 6:30 at daycare of their grandmother's house, so I could begin work my 7:00 a.m. I work 10 hours a day for four days each week. After work, like any mother, I picked up my children and headed home to prepare dinner. While dinner is being prepared, I juggle entertaining my son while helping my daughter with homework.

## Motivation for Mompreneurs

*All the while*, a nap or just resting my feet would be on my mind. Once the children ate dinner, I would spend time playing "hide and seek" or "church" with them - and trying to find way to market BadChick. There were times I would pause a game with the children because I was on a call concerning a speaking engagement, trying to come up with more ways to grow my business, or taking trainings via web or conference call. By 7:30 p.m., the children got their baths. Every night at 8:00 p.m., they are in bed. We would say our prayers and then lights **OUT**!

Now, at this time, you would think I would enjoy some "me-time". Not exactly. As ready as I would be for a hot shower, my legs didn't carry me to the bathroom, so I waited until morning to shower. I would make attempts to end my night in much-needed prayer, but quickly fall asleep after "*Lord, I truly thank you for another day...*"

## Compiled by Dr. M.E. Porter

I spent so much time trying to maintain my family, my job, **and** my own business, I put myself on the backburner. I put everything before myself to the point that I lacked energy to do anything I enjoyed. I would be completely overwhelmed with all of my responsibilities. I realized I lacked a support staff. My family was there to watch over my children on certain occasions, but not everyone was local. What I needed was *business* support.

I play every role in BadChick. I am the Founder. I am a Motivational Speaker. I am an Author. I am Public Relations. I am my own Vendor. I am my Assistant. The list goes on. I even travel alone. *Jesus knows.. I get SO exhausted.*

**Whew, Lordy!** Multitasking. Is it really at its best when you're that stressed out? Nope! Not at all. The imbalance in my life, family, and work was unhealthy.

On the weekends when I didn't have any speaking engagements, I would try my best to get my children to go in their rooms and play so I could begin the next book outline or work on a way to market BadChick. If all children are like mine, you can't just ignore them. *Haha!* They are going to tell you what they have to say - whether you're on the phone doing work, or not.

Really, I was so busy putting more time into my business than my children on weekends. It wasn't a great feeling at all. I could tell they noticed the lack of attention. I had to learn that family remains first. I had to learn that I can't do it all. I had to learn to say 'no' to certain engagements.

I quickly learned I can **never** reschedule precious time with my children, but I can **always** reschedule an event, meeting, or training. Learning to prioritize is so important. As Mompreneurs, we must make sacrifices and compromises. We have to learn to effectively multitask. We can't do everything ourselves. As independent as we want to be, everyone needs help. We cannot be too proud to seek help in areas where we may need it; it may be help with our business tasks or help with our children. Now, that's **not** to say being a Mompreneur will become rainbows and unicorns; but having balance will give us peace and rest that is needed amongst the many circumstances of everyday life.

Mostly, I learned to remain in God. When I lack anything, I learned to not seek it anywhere but in God. I had to learn to find time for rest. That rest could be napping - but my **greatest** rest came from resting at the feet of Christ. I had to learn to listen to Him concerning what I needed to be doing. I had to ask for help with balance. I had to ask what it was I needed to eliminate.

## Motivation for Mompreneurs

I *love* the following two scriptures:

1. *"A false balance and dishonest business practices are extremely offensive to the Lord, but an accurate scale is His delight"* (Proverbs 11:1, AMP).

2. *"There is a season (a time appointed) for everything and a time for every delight and event or purpose under Heaven - A time to be born and a time to die; a time to plant and a time to uproot what is planted. A time to kill and a time to heal; a time to tear down and a time to build up. A time to weep and a time to laugh; a time to mourn and a time to dance. A time to throw away stones and a time to gather stones; a time to embrace and a time to refrain from embracing. A time to search and a time to give up as lost; a time to keep and a time to throw away. A time to tear apart and a time to sew together; a time to keep silent and a time to speak. A time to love and a time to hate; a time for war and a time for peace. What profit is there for the worker from that in which he labors? I have seen the task which God has given to the sons of men with which to occupy themselves"* (Ecclesiastes 3:1-10, AMP).

You see, **God** makes the appointed time for everything. He gives us the tasks we are to occupy ourselves with. If it's motherhood tasks, then listening to the Father is what we should do. If it's a speaking engagement or time writing the next book, then listening to the Father is what we should do. Just the same, if it's a time when we should refrain from embracing certain opportunities or tasks, then He knows best. There is a time for *everything*. There is a season for *everything*. There is **no** imbalance in Christ.

Lastly, there are four things we can immediately apply to our lives:

- ➤ Do what we love to do.
- ➤ Make our business a family affair by finding ways to include our children.
- ➤ Embrace any failures because they are learning-opportunities in both business **and** motherhood.
- ➤ Seek solace (comfort, support, and relief).

Be encouraged today, my sisters! God bless you!

*"She makes linen garments and sells them, and supplies sashes for the merchants."*
Proverbs 31:24

My name is Sharon Covington Shamburger. I was born and raised in Asheboro, North Carolina where I currently reside. I am a 29-year-old wife and mother of two beautiful children: Londyn and Masiah. I graduated from Southern Guilford High School in 2006. August 10, 2014 was the day I gave my life to Christ. I am truly a woman after God's own heart.

My passion is deliverance ministry. Truly, I desire for God to use me to be a blessing to others. I am the CEO and Founder of BAD CHICK (Blessed And Delivered Choosing Happiness In Christ's Kingdom). November 23, 2016 - my 29th birthday - my first book titled *B.A.D. (Blessed and Delivered)* was published. Learn more by visiting:
www.badchickbysharon.info

Compiled by Dr. M.E. Porter

*"Fear not, for I am with you; be not dismayed, for I am your God; I will strengthen you, I will help you, I will uphold you with My righteous right hand."*
Isaiah 41:10

Relax...and have a girls' night out with good friends.

## Juggling Fitness and Being a Single Mom
By Mary D. Powe

Being a working woman/single parent, how do you juggle work, build a business, **and** take care of home? I am a single mother, full of life and ambition, with three *amazing* children.

My dreams took a turn for the worse in 2014 because I had to face the challenges of not being able to walk due to a Sciatic nerve occurrence. After accepting the diagnosis, wrapping my mind around the fact that I can't move to provide for my family, and not having a means of revenue, it took me to a place no single mother wants to visit.

My struggle and determination had allowed me to teach myself how to walk again. That gave me the opportunity to help other ladies who felt helpless and hopeless in their own struggles, while overcoming adversity.

As a personal trainer, I take pride in teaching ladies how to deal with the challenges that will take place in their lives, as well as build self-esteem and transform their bodies. My strength, guidance, and desire go a long way to help determined working women on the go. I help women realize their potential for becoming better-suited to handle the challenges that daily life can present.

As a single parent, Mompreneur, and fitness instructor, I focus on continual learning by teaching and empowering clients with the knowledge, skills, and support to inspire ladies to live a healthier life. Together, we actively participate in regular fitness activities and integrate nutrition to make their health goals a reality. My goal is to help women ease into a healthy and active lifestyle in a caring, fun, and dynamic atmosphere.

# Motivation for Mompreneurs

I am an Aerobic Instructor, Personal Trainer, and Boot Camp Coordinator. I am also the Owner of Get It Done Fitness with Mary. I specialize in helping today's busy moms find balance and have the energy to tackle other hectic schedules. I majored in Physical Education at the University of Southern Mississippi, becoming a Certified Trainer in 2015.

I am the Founder and Host of "Fitness Corner" on Facebook Live. By sharing my knowledge and experience on this platform, it allows ladies to be unguarded and transparent. Also, I reach ladies near and far, helping them to engage and empower themselves by giving simple solutions to their complex lives.

Some ladies are suffering from low self-esteem and are still harboring feelings of disappointment, anger, and blame. That's why I cater to ladies who can identify with these issues and not be afraid to be transparent about their lives. My progress and determination gives ladies someone they **know** will fight for them to have a more meaningful life. The programs offered help women release some of the stress that comes with the feelings of being unworthy, unattractive, and unappreciated. By showing up for women who can't stand up for themselves, I give them a little light at the end of the tunnel!

*"She extends her hand to the poor,*
*Yes, she reaches out her hands to the needy."*
Proverbs 31:20

## Dedication

RaShod, Jakobe, and KeAsya:

**YOU ALL** are the love of my life.

Compiled by Dr. M.E. Porter

Mary D. Powe, The Fitness Diva

Aerobics Instructor, Personal Trainer, and Boot Camp Coordinator.
Learn more by visiting:
www.facebook.com/mary.d.powe

## MOMPRENEUR MOTIVATOR

"Forget all the reasons it won't work and believe the one reason that it will."

~ Unknown ~

Compiled by Dr. M.E. Porter

## The Corns Speak
By Angela R. Edwards

*Rain. Sleet. Snow. Or shine.*

It didn't matter: **I had to take care of mine.**

My struggle as a Mompreneur came by way of working a "9 to 5" job, five days a week. Nothing extraordinary there, right? That's what Mompreneurs do! *However*, my struggle included drudging through rain, sleet, snow, or shine...on foot...a half mile one way...for **four** years. My attendance record was virtually flawless. I was dedicated and laser-focused on showing up and showing out daily - and taking care of my children.

I can recall days when I would make the trek to work, and co-workers would drive past me, honk, wave…and keep going. I **wanted** to be angry with them. I **wanted** to lay them *OUT* with the power of my words for not thinking enough of me to pull over and give me a ride. Peace came to my spirit when God reminded me, "*You're **my** child. I will always take care of you.*"

Okay, God. I hear you. **BUT REALLY!** These corns on my baby toes are *killing* me.

*"Hush, my child. I will never leave you nor forsake you."*

I can't fail to mention this *one* unique aspect of my Mompreneurship: I was living with a man who didn't work a steady job for the entirety of our relationship. I'm **sure** I'm not the only one to ever play the fool for the sake of a warm body to lay next to... I should have been ashamed of myself, but I wasn't - at least not in the moment. I did what I had to do for my **CHILDREN**: I always have and always will until the Good Lord calls me home. I worked and made that trek for four years because my **CHILDREN** needed to eat, needed a roof over their heads, needed clothes, etc., etc. As the one tasked with the gift of being a mother, I gave my two children all I had to give - corns on the toes and all that came with it. The struggle was real.

## Motivation for Mompreneurs

To be honest, I have learned to see the positive in the negative. It was a lesson I learned from my mother, and I am grateful for her wisdom. A few of the positives were:

1. My children learned the responsibilities of being a parent by the way I modeled parenting.

2. I was so physically-fit from all of that walking, I once had a man with "Jungle Fever" tell me I had the body of Tennis Great, Serena Williams *(yes, the hourglass figure and shapely calves were on and poppin')!*

3. In due time, the so-called man I was with had to acknowledge I was a "Wonder Woman", as he "wondered" why I put up with his lack for so long.

Always mindful that God would **never** leave me nor forsake me, the time came for me to get rid of the zero and make *MYSELF* the hero. My level of motivation for caring for my two children never left; however, that **third** child - that grown man who was comfortable having a woman take care of him - had to **GO**. I will admit that I was fearful of being alone, yet I was lonely in the relationship because he was falling short at every turn. He had to **GO**. I will also admit I was comfy for one day too long with his shenanigans: me at work, him roaming the streets doing *nothing* productive with his time. He had to **GO**.

Ladies, I have "been there, done that" - with no desire to go back. Strange thing: As I sit here penning my story, I just had an "AH HA!" moment. I never put together why that man was **so** comfortable not stepping up to be a man…until now. His very own mother did the exact same thing I did. She held down the household. She worked her fingers to the bone to ensure her four children *never* lacked. And she did it while **HER** husband sat at home doing - you guessed it! - *nothing*.

Wow, God! That was **DEEP**! I suppose there **IS** truth when it is said our children do what they *SEE*.

Wow, God! Just…wow.

Anyway, as a Momprenuer, I am happy to say I am now happily-married to a **MAN**. I don't walk anywhere any longer - unless I'm exercising or walking my dog. I work from home and frequent my office when I desire - not because I **HAVE** to. *Who am I?* I am Angela Edwards, the CEO of Pearly Gates Publishing LLC, a Christian Book Publisher based out of Houston, Texas. I now pour my all into my clients and their literary arts while my husband goes to work five days a week and works **LONG** days with the airlines.

When I *feel* like **I'M** falling short at every turn, my husband gently and lovingly reminds me that we are empty-nesters and that I'm doing more than enough. I absolutely *love* when he tells me, "Keep your money in your pocket" or "Go buy yourself something nice". **Whaaaat?** He doesn't get an argument out of me!

I feel like I did my bid. I proved to myself, my children, and to God that I am responsible and willing to do what it takes to be the woman **HE** designed me to be. Today, my children are grown with children of their own. Both of them are productive members of society and phenomenal parents. I have no doubt they would sacrifice their baby toes for their children if they had to, but alas, *THEIR* days are bright and sunny.

*I give myself a high-five - and a **HALLELUJAH SHOUT** to God*

*Rain, sleet, snow, and shine.*

**All glory to God: I took care of mine.**

> *"She is not afraid of snow for her household,*
> *for all her household is clothed with scarlet."*
> Proverbs 31:21

Compiled by Dr. M.E. Porter

## Dedication to Anequilla and Gerald

To my two loves. To my two ride-or-dies. To my two babies. To NiNi and ManMan. I love you with all the love a mother can muster up for her children. I love you with the love of Christ and pray for you always. Your names are on my lips when I rise and when I lay down for rest, as I ask our Heavenly Father to keep watch over you and your children all the days of our lives.

Special love to 'Niyah, Phat-Phat, Batman, and KoKo Bean. Raise my grandbabies knowing the love of Christ. They are never too young to learn about Him!

Woman of God. Wife. Mother. Sister. Friend.

CEO of Pearly Gates Publishing LLC, a low-cost Christian Book Publisher.

Founder of the Battle-Scar Free Movement and the Trumpet for Change for Domestic Violence victims and survivors.

Administrative Director for Motivational Outreach Ministers and Mentors.

Learn more by visiting:
www.pearlygatespublishing.com

Compiled by Dr. M.E. Porter

*"The God who equipped me with strength and made my way blameless. He made my feet like the feet of a deer and set me secure on the heights. He trains my hands for war, so that my arms can bend a bow of bronze."*
Psalm 18:32-34

Relax...snuggle up with a blanket, and have a Netflix marathon.

## MOMPRENEUR MOTIVATOR

"I am thankful for all of those who said NO to me. It's because of them, I'm doing it myself."

~ Albert Einstein ~

Compiled by Dr. M.E. Porter

# CONTACT DR. MARILYN E. PORTER

FOR BOOKINGS, CONTACT
DR. PORTER VIA EMAIL:
INFO@MARILYNEPORTER.COM

Compiled by Dr. M.E. Porter

## OTHER M.E. PORTER TITLES

### IF YOU ENJOYED THIS BOOK, HERE ARE OTHER M.E. PORTER TITLES:

*The Pieces of ME (And YOU)*

*HERstory Reveals His Glory*

*Though I Walk (Divine Healing in the Valley)*

*Affirmations & Antidotes That Remind ME*

### ***COMING IN 2017***

*Stories from The Pink Pulpit* (June)

*By the Still Waters* (July)

*Affirmations That Heal ME* (September)

www.ingramcontent.com/pod-product-compliance
Lightning Source LLC
Chambersburg PA
CBHW071530080526
44588CB00011B/1630